Union Public Library

W9-AOX-810

Paul Revere

A Buddy Book
by
Sarah Tieck

ABDO
Publishing Company

Union Public Library

VISIT US AT
www.abdopublishing.com

Published by ABDO Publishing Company, 4940 Viking Drive, Suite 622, Edina, Minnesota 55435. Copyright © 2007 by Abdo Consulting Group, Inc. International copyrights reserved in all countries. No part of this book may be reproduced in any form without written permission from the publisher.

Printed in the United States.

Contributing Editor: Michael P. Goecke
Graphic Design: Jane Halbert
Cover Photograph: Library of Congress
Interior Photographs/Illustrations: Clipart.com, Getty Images, Hulton Archives, Library of Congress, North Wind, Photodisc

Library of Congress Cataloging-in-Publication Data

Tieck, Sarah, 1976–
   Paul Revere / Sarah Tieck.
     p. cm. — (First biographies. Set V)
   Includes index.
   ISBN 10 1-59679-787-8
   ISBN 13 978-1-59679-787-1
   1. Revere, Paul, 1735–1818—Juvenile literature. 2. Statesmen—Massachusetts—Biography—Juvenile literature. 3. Massachusetts—Biography—Juvenile literature. 4. Massachusetts—History—Revolution, 1775–1783—Juvenile literature. I. Title II. Series: Gosda, Randy T, 1959– . First biographies. Set V.

F69.R43T54 2006
973.3'311092—dc22

                                       2005031970

Table Of Contents

Who Is Paul Revere? 4

Paul's Family...6

Growing Up 8

A Family Man 10

A Business Man 12

A Patriot 14

Paul's Famous Ride..16

Fighting For Independence 24

After The Revolution.......................................26

A Productive Life 28

Important Dates...30

Important Words...31

Web Sites 31

Index 32

Who Is Paul Revere?

    Paul Revere was an American patriot. He lived during the American Revolutionary War. At this time, America was made up of 13 colonies. The colonies were ruled by Great Britain.

    Many colonists were unhappy with Great Britain. They did not like paying high British taxes. The colonists wanted to be free of British rule. They wanted to form their own country.

    Paul helped in the fight for independence. Paul Revere helped America became a strong country.

The 13 Colonies In 1776

Massachusetts (District of Maine)

New Hampshire

Massachusetts

Rhode Island

Connecticut

New York

Pennsylvania

New Jersey

Delaware

North America

Virginia

Maryland

North Carolina

South Carolina

Georgia

The 13 original colonies were ruled by Great Britain.

Paul's Family

Paul Revere was born in Boston, Massachusetts, in December 1734. No one knows the exact date.

Paul's mother was Deborah Revere. Paul's father was also named Paul Revere.

Paul's mother was from Boston. Paul's father came to America from France. In France, Paul's father had a different name. His French name was Apollos Rivoire. He changed his name in America so it was easier for people to say.

A view of Boston in the 1700s.
This is when Paul lived there.

Growing Up

The Revere family lived in Boston. It is believed that Paul had between nine and 12 brothers and sisters.

Paul's mother took care of the children and the house. Paul's father was a silversmith and goldsmith. He made things out of silver and gold.

Paul was the second child and the oldest son. He went to school at the North Writing School in Boston. Also, Paul was his father's apprentice. Paul's father taught him how to make things from silver and gold.

Paul and his father worked together in a shop like this one.

In 1754, Paul's father died. Paul had to take care of his family. In 1756, when Paul was 19, he became a soldier. He fought in the French and Indian War.

A Family Man

After the war, Paul got married and started a family. He married Sarah Orne in 1757. Sarah and Paul had eight children.

Paul's wife died in 1773. Paul missed Sarah very much. But, he needed help to take care of the children.

Paul got married again in 1773. His second wife was named Rachel Walker. Rachel helped take care of Paul's children and his home. They were married for many years. Paul and Rachel had eight children, too.

A view of Paul's house in Boston.

A Business Man

Working with silver and gold made Paul strong. He had to pound the metal with a hammer. Paul also had to make designs and cut the pieces.

Paul worked very hard. He and his apprentices made spoons, tea sets, and other things. Paul put his name "Revere" or "P.R." on each piece he made.

Paul worked his whole life as a silversmith and a goldsmith. He made many things. He was known for his skill. People still remember Paul's work. Some of his pieces can still be seen today.

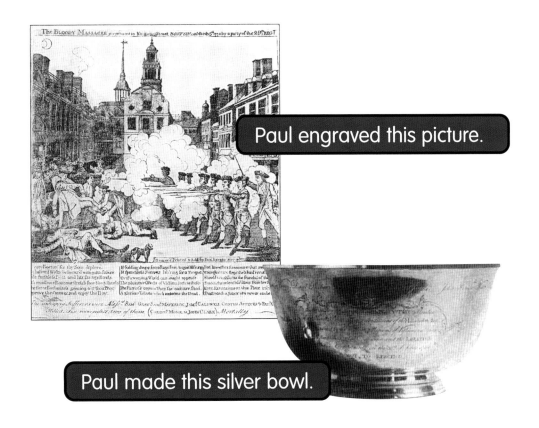

Paul engraved this picture.

Paul made this silver bowl.

But, he had other businesses. He printed political cartoons. He made pictures for books and magazines. He worked as a dentist. And, he also ran a hardware store.

A Patriot

Paul had many friends in the business community. He and his friends wanted to change things. They wanted to help America become a country.

Paul and his friends were patriots. They watched the British soldiers. They had secret meetings. They shared important information with other patriots.

A view of the Boston Tea Party.

On the night of December 16, 1773, Paul and some other colonists went aboard the British ships. They dumped 342 chests filled with tea into Boston Harbor. They did this to protest the British government. This is known as the Boston Tea Party.

Paul's Famous Ride

In 1774 and 1775, Paul worked as an express rider for the patriots. He delivered messages and news to people on horse. Sometimes, he rode all the way to New York from Boston.

On the night of April 18, 1775, a man named Dr. Joseph Warren talked to Paul. He asked Paul to ride to Lexington, Massachusetts.

Paul delivered information to many people.

The British soldiers were going to Lexington to arrest Samuel Adams and John Hancock. These men were leaders of the patriots. The soldiers had been ordered by King George III to stop the patriots. They were also supposed to destroy their supplies. Dr. Warren wanted Paul to warn Adams and Hancock.

Paul found out the British were coming by sea. So, colonists hung two lanterns in the bell tower of Christ Church. This was a special signal to warn the other patriots.

Two lanterns hung in the bell tower of Christ Church. This meant the British soldiers were coming by sea.

Paul rode in a boat across the Charles River.

Paul left Boston around 10:00 PM. Two friends took him across the Charles River on their boat. On the other side, Paul borrowed a horse. Then, Paul rode to Lexington as fast as he could. On the way, he stopped to warn people that British soldiers were coming.

At midnight, Paul arrived at the house where Samuel Adams and John Hancock were staying. Paul delivered his message. Two other riders arrived with the same message as Paul. Their names were William Dawes and Dr. Samuel Prescott. The three men went together to save supplies in the nearby town of Concord.

Adams and Hancock stayed in this house.

On the way, the British captured Paul. When the soldiers let him go, they took his horse. Paul went to Lexington anyway. He met up with Adams and Hancock. They left together. Later, Paul went back to Lexington to save some important papers. When he arrived, the patriots were fighting the British.

Paul was captured by British soldiers.

Fighting For Independence

In 1775, America and Britain went to war. This is called the American Revolutionary War. In 1776, Benjamin Franklin helped Thomas Jefferson write the Declaration of Independence. With this, America broke away from Great Britain.

Many battles were fought during the American Revolutionary War.

Paul went to war to help fight for America, too. At the start of the war, he made gunpowder. Paul also made brass cannons for the army.

In 1778 and 1779, Paul commanded troops in Massachusetts and Maine. He also fought in some battles. But, things didn't go well. So, Paul left the military.

In 1783, America won the American Revolutionary War. America became a free country.

After The Revolution

Paul returned to his family's business after serving in the war. He became known for his products and ideas. During the war, he created and printed the first paper money for the United States. Also, he made a state seal for Massachusetts. This seal is still used today.

Around 1788, Paul and his sons opened a foundry. The foundry made nails, bolts, and cannons. In 1792, they started making bells. Paul made a bell for King's Chapel in Boston. It still rings today.

After the war, the United States still had to buy copper sheets from England. Paul wanted the United States to make its own copper sheets. This is why he opened a copper-rolling mill in 1801. It was the first one in the country.

Paul's mill made copper sheets for the USS *Constitution*. This ship is still in Boston Harbor.

The USS *Constitution* was also called "Old Ironsides." It is a famous battleship.

A Productive Life

Paul retired in 1811. He was 76. His sons took over his businesses. In 1813, Paul Revere's wife Rachel died. He was very sad. Paul died on May 10, 1818. He was 83.

Americans have not forgotten Paul Revere. He is remembered as an American hero. There are statues to honor him. There is even a poem about Paul's famous ride. This was written by a poet named Henry Wadsworth Longfellow in 1860.

This is a statue of Paul Revere in Boston.

Important Dates

December 1734 Paul Revere is born. No one knows the exact date.

1756 Paul fights in the French and Indian War.

1757 Paul marries Sarah Orne.

1773 Sarah dies. Paul marries Rachel Walker.

December 16, 1773 Paul helps with the Boston Tea Party.

April 18, 1775 Paul rides to Lexington to warn people that the British are coming.

1775 The American Revolutionary War begins.

1783 America wins the American Revolutionary War.

1788 Paul and his sons open a foundry.

1801 Paul and his sons open the first U. S. copper-rolling mill.

1811 Paul retires.

1813 Rachel dies.

May 10, 1818 Paul Revere dies.

Important Words

American Revolutionary War the war Americans fought to win their freedom from Britain. It lasted from 1775 to 1783.

apprentice a person who learns a trade or craft by helping a skilled worker.

colony a settlement. Colonists are the people who live in a colony.

Declaration of Independence an important paper in American history. In it, Americans say they are ready to break away from Britain and rule themselves as a free, or independent, country.

French and Indian War a war that started in America and continued in Europe between 1754 and 1763.

goldsmith a skilled worker who makes things out of gold. A silversmith makes things out of silver.

independence to be free from someone or something.

patriot someone who loves their country.

tax money charged by a city or country.

Web Sites

To learn more about Paul Revere, visit ABDO Publishing Company on the World Wide Web. Web site links about Paul Revere are featured on our Book Links page. These links are routinely monitored and updated to provide the most current information available.

www.abdopublishing.com

Index

Adams, Samuel **18, 21, 22**

American Revolutionary
   War **4,
   24, 25, 26, 27, 30**

Boston, Massachusetts . .**6, 7,
   8, 11, 15, 16, 20, 26, 29, 30**

Boston Harbor **15**

Boston Tea Party **15, 30**

Charles River **20**

Christ Church **18, 19**

Concord, Massachusetts . . .**21**

Dawes, William **21**

Declaration of
   Independence **24**

France **6**

Franklin, Benjamin **24**

French and Indian War . .**9, 30**

George III (King of
   England) **18**

Great Britain . .**4, 5, 18, 24, 27**

Hancock, John **18, 21, 22**

Jefferson, Thomas **24**

King's Chapel **26**

Lexington, Massachusetts . .**16,
   18, 20, 22, 30**

Longfellow, Henry
   Wadsworth **28**

Maine **25**

Massachusetts **6,
   16, 25, 26**

New York **16**

North Writing School **8**

Orne, Sarah **10, 30**

Prescott, Samuel **21**

Revere, Deborah **6, 8, 9**

Rivoire, Apollos **6, 8, 9**

USS *Constitution* **27**

Walker, Rachel **10, 28, 30**

Warren, Joseph **16, 18**